Prayers we have in common

Agreed Liturgical Texts Proposed By
The International Consultation on English Texts

Enlarged and Revised Edition

GEOFFREY CHAPMAN
LONDON   1971

Geoffrey Chapman
18 High Street, Wimbledon, London SW19

Geoffrey Chapman (Ireland)
5–7 Main Street, Blackrock, County Dublin

ISBN 0 225 48936 8

First edition published 1970
Revised, enlarged edition published June 1971
Reprinted October 1971

This book is set in 11/13pt Press Roman (IBM) by
Claire Graphics, Wimbledon, SW19.

Printed in Great Britain by
Lowe & Brydone (Printers) Ltd., London

Contents

Foreword

There exists in the Roman Catholic Church a body known as ICEL or the International Committee on English in the Liturgy, whose task it is "to achieve an English version of liturgical texts acceptable to the interested countries...bearing in mind the ecumenical aspects". In recent years the Advisory Committee of this body has been meeting with representatives of the major Christian Churches throughout the English-speaking world; and from these discussions there emerged the conviction that it would be possible to produce agreed versions of a number of liturgical texts which could be used by everyone. A great deal of work towards this end was done by groups in Great Britain, America, Australia and elsewhere: and this preliminary work was collected and reviewed by an international and ecumenical body which has been established and which is known as the International Consultation on English Texts. This body has been meeting since 1969; and in the following year it produced two sets of texts. These were published in the first edition of *Prayers We Have in Common*. The first contained texts which had been under discussion by various groups for some considerable time and on which the Consultation had reached agreement. The second contained drafts on which the Consultation was still working. This work has now been completed.

All the completed texts, together with notes, are now presented in this book: and the Consultation hopes that the Christian Churches of the English-speaking world will be prepared to use these experimentally over an extended period. The reception accorded to the first set of texts published in 1970 has been encouraging: and a number of Churches have already undertaken to use them.

It is our earnest hope that all the texts now available will be found acceptable for use both in public worship and in private prayer and that they will make a modest contribution to the cause of Christian unity.

Ronald Jasper $\Big\}$ Joint Chairmen of ICET
Harold Winstone

THE LORD'S PRAYER

1. Our Father in heaven,
2.   holy be your Name,
3.   your kingdom come,
4.   your will be done,
5.   on earth as in heaven.
6. Give us today our daily bread.
7. Forgive us our sins
8.   as we forgive those who sin against us.
9. Do not bring us to the test
10.   but deliver us from evil.

11. For the kingdom, the power, and the glory are yours
12.   now and for ever.

    The Lord's Prayer lies at the heart of Christian devotion; and it is laden with rich personal and traditional associations. Change therefore prompts all kinds of reactions. But change is no new thing in the history of this prayer; and today no single invariable version is in common use throughout the English-speaking world. Comparison of the text of St Matthew 6:9ff. in the King James (Authorised) Version of the Bible with the version in the Anglican Book of Common Prayer of 1662 at once reveals differences: and such variations may serve to remind us that between our current and familiar versions and the Greek text of the prayer as recorded in the New Testament stand earlier English renderings and an even earlier Latin translation. To retranslate the Lord's Prayer for a new situation is no new procedure. It should also be emphasised that in the task of producing translations the Church has never been in the position of working from and with one fixed "original" text. It is clear that the Greek texts of the prayer as preserved in the Gospels are themselves a "translation" from Hebrew or Aramaic: and the texts which appear in St Matthew and St Luke do not agree. The extent

of the divergence is clear from the following quotations
(taken from the Revised Standard Version).

Matthew 6:9–13	*Luke* 11:2–4
Our Father who art in heaven,	Father
Hallowed be thy name.	Hallowed be thy name.
Thy kingdom come,	Thy kingdom come.
Thy will be done,	
On earth as it is in heaven.	
Give us this day our daily	Give us each day our daily
bread;	bread;
And forgive us our debts,	And forgive us our sins,
As we also have forgiven	For we ourselves forgive
our debtors;	everyone who is indebted
	to us;
And lead us not into	And lead us not into
temptation,	temptation.
But deliver us from evil.	

The new translation submitted for experimental use is based
on the Greek text of St Matthew's Gospel, since this has
always been the basis of the Church's liturgical tradition. It
retains the style and even the words of the familiar version so
far as this is consistent with the elimination of archaic ex-
pressions and with the demands of clear and accurate
translation.

Line 2. *Holy be your Name.* This may be a petition or it may
be a doxology. If it is a doxology, it refers to the preceding
line rather than the two which follow it, and it is parallel to
such Jewish acclamations as "The Holy One, *blessed be He*".
If it is a petition, it should be taken in conjunction with the
lines that succeed it. Then it has a profound eschatological
significance and is a prayer that something be *done*—whether
by God or man. There are weighty reasons for thinking that
what is being sought is the action of God; and in that event
the whole opening section of the prayer would represent an
urgent seeking for the great eschatological deed of God to be

executed and revealed—"Father: show yourself to be the Holy One: bring in your kingdom; establish your will; on earth as in heaven". Nevertheless, reference to similar Jewish usage reveals that a strong case can be made for viewing the petitions as referring to human action, and as embodying the prayer that men may so act that God's Name may be sanctified, his kingdom established, and his will accomplished.

No absolute and exclusive decision on this line of the prayer can fairly be made. Ideally the translation should allow the whole breadth of interpretation whether doxological or petitionary for the action of God and/or man. "Your Name be hallowed" is probably the translation which keeps most of the options open; but the word "hallowed" has apparently passed out of currency or become debased, at least in some parts of the English-speaking world. Accordingly "holy be your Name" is proposed, though with the realisation that it tends to swing the interpretative emphasis towards the doxological understanding.

Line 6. *Give us today our daily bread.* The translation "daily bread" is notoriously uncertain. It may mean "bread for tomorrow", referring not only to the next day but also the "great tomorrow", or the final consummation. The petition would then be for the food of the heavenly banquet; and this would fit well with the eschatological perspective which seems to control the whole of the prayer. On the other hand it could mean simply "the bread which is necessary", without any particular temporal reference. There would seem to be no sufficient reason for substantially varying the familiar translation.

Lines 7–8. *Forgive us our sins as we forgive those who sin against us.* "Sins" and "sin" have been used to convey the sense, while avoiding the narrow connotation of "trespasses" and "trespass", and even "debts" and "debtors".

Line 9. *Do not bring us to the test.* Two errors must be avoided in this line. The first is the misconception that God can be the agent of temptation: the second is that the original Greek word means "temptation" as it is meant today. The reference here is primarily eschatological. It is probably a petition for deliverance from the final "time of trial" which, in biblical thought, marks the Last Days and the full revelation of anti-Christ. The peril envisaged is that of apostasy—the renunciation of the Christian faith in the face of the suffering and persecution which is expected to herald the final triumph of God's Kingdom (cf. Luke 22:31, 32, 40; Revelation 3:10). Yet a reference to any occasion of testing, when issues of life and death are in the balance, is not excluded. Either way, it is certainly not subjective moral temptations that are basically envisaged. The suggested translation seems to be the most adequate available.

Lines 11-12. *For the kingdom, the power, and the glory are yours now and for ever.* The presence of these words in many Greek manuscripts, even if not the earliest and most reliable ones, reflects the Jewish practice of concluding prayers of petition with a doxology of praise. This formula has enjoyed a wide and long use, and it is liturgically appropriate. Its presence is therefore to be commended.

THE APOSTLES' CREED

1. I believe in God, the Father almighty,
2.   creator of heaven and earth.

3. I believe in Jesus Christ, his only Son, our Lord.
4.   He was conceived by the power of the Holy Spirit
5.   and born of the Virgin Mary.
6.   He suffered under Pontius Pilate,
7.   was crucified, died, and was buried.
8.   He descended to the dead.
9.   On the third day he rose again.
10.   He ascended into heaven,
11.   and is seated at the right hand of the Father.
12.   He will come again to judge the living and the dead.

13. I believe in the Holy Spirit,
14.   the holy catholic Church,
15.   the communion of saints,
16.   the forgiveness of sins,
17.   the resurrection of the body,
18.   and the life everlasting.

The Latin text upon which this proposed translation is based first appeared in documents of the eighth century; but it is clearly related to texts of earlier origin. The primary associations of this creed were with baptism; and the more individual form of a baptismal creed is reflected in its use of the first person singular and its lack of a final "Amen".

Line 2. *creator*. This is suggested as a correct translation of the Latin *"creatorem"*, in contrast to "maker" in the Nicene Creed—*poiétén*.

Line 8. This line is made a separate theological assertion, independent of the assertions in lines 7 and 9. It is a difficult line to interpret. Some have understood it as underlying the assertion of death. Others, following 1 Peter 3:19, have thought of our Lord proclaiming his victory to the souls of the departed. While others have thought of our Lord going to battle with Satan, and in so doing guaranteeing the deliverance of the saints. Since all these contain the idea of going to the place of the dead, the Latin *ad inferna* is translated "to the dead". The figure of descent has been retained, since it is part of the total metaphor used in the creed.

Line 10. *ascended* is retained for the same reason and because the biblical picture of which it is a part seems unavoidable. The Ascension also has a fixed place in the Church's calendar.

Line 11. *the Father.* To reiterate the first line's "God, the Father almighty" makes the line unnecessarily ponderous.

Line 14. *catholic.* This word is richer than any possible substitutes, e.g. "universal", and it is the common use of English-speaking Churches.

Line 15. *communion of saints.* The latin *sanctorum communionem* could mean either a fellowship of holy people or a participation in holy things, e.g. the sacraments. The former concept is adopted, not only because of its traditional use, but also because the Consultation felt that it was not within its terms of reference to attempt to decide an issue which is still under discussion.

THE NICENE CREED

1. We believe in one God,
2.   the Father, the Almighty,
3.   maker of heaven and earth,
4.   of all that is seen and unseen.

5. We believe in one Lord, Jesus Christ,
6.   the only Son of God,
7.   eternally begotten of the Father,
8.   God from God, Light from Light,
9.   true God from true God,
10.   begotten, not made, one in Being with the Father.
11.   Through him all things were made.
12.   For us men and for our salvation
13.   he came down from heaven:
14.   by the power of the Holy Spirit
15.   he was born of the Virgin Mary, and became man.
16.   For our sake he was crucified under Pontius Pilate;
17.   he suffered, died, and was buried.
18.   On the third day he rose again
19.   in fulfilment of the Scriptures;
20.   he ascended into heaven
21.   and is seated at the right hand of the Father.
22.   He will come again in glory to judge the living and the
                                                            dead,
23.   and his kingdom will have no end.

24. We believe in the Holy Spirit, the Lord, the giver of life,
25.   who proceeds from the Father (and the Son).
26.   With the Father and the Son he is worshipped and
                                                    glorified.
27.   He has spoken through the Prophets.
28.   We believe in one holy catholic and apostolic Church.
29.   We acknowledge one baptism for the forgiveness of
                                                        sins.
30.   We look for the resurrection of the dead,
31.   and the life of the world to come. Amen.

This creed is an ancient statement of belief which requires correct translation rather than paraphrase. An attempt has been made to achieve simplicity and clarity without losing any point of theological significance.

Line 1. *We believe.* The use of the plural "we" follows the Greek text of the original conciliar form of credal statement. It is appropriate in a creed spoken by the whole congregation and is distinct from the use of the singular in the Apostles' Creed, which had its origin in a personal profession of faith. This use of the plural, however, does not preclude its being also a personal profession of faith, just as in the case of the Gloria or of collects.

Line 2. *the Almighty.* The article is added to bring out the significance of the Greek *pantocrator,* which is a noun and not an adjective, and is the Septuagint rendering of the Hebrew divine name (cf. Revelation 1:8 and 4:8).

Line 3. *seen and unseen.* This refers to "heaven and earth" in the previous line and not to some further acts of creation. While the reference is thus to such things as angels, it should not preclude the notion of further creative processes as being part of the divine plan. These words were also considered to be easier to sing than "visible and invisible".

Line 5. *We believe.* The repetition of this phrase for stylistic reasons is found in several early creeds.

Lines 6–10. *begotten.* This word occurs three times in the Greek to describe the Son's unique relationship with the Father as distinct from the mere process of birth. The Latin text dropped the formal equivalent in line 7 (*genitum*), and has *natum ex Patre* which seems less appropriate than its use of *natus* with *Maria* in the Apostles' Creed, or the use of "born" in the new English version of line 15. Twice was also considered to be sufficient to use *begotten* in English: it was dropped in line 6 as unnecessary and was restored in line 7 to distinguish the truth conveyed by the Greek from any idea that the Son was created in time, or alternatively born in eternity. "Born" is still needed to describe his incarnation in time and is correctly used in line 15.

Line 7. *eternally begotten.* In spite of some dissatisfaction with this phrase, no better alternative has been suggested. There are certain philosophical objections to the recent proposal "before time began"; while the older phrase "before all worlds" was felt to be too obscure and archaic. The phrase represents one of those statements in the original creed of Nicaea that was specifically anti-Arian, directed at the denial of the Son's eternity and the assertion of his posteriority to the Father. Those who find that the adverb "eternally" is too suggestive of an "ongoing process" may be referred to J.N.D. Kelly's *Early Christian Doctrine* (2nd ed. p. 243), where he points out that St Athanasius argued that "the Son must exist eternally alongside the Father. The explanation of this is that His generation is an eternal process": see also his *Early Christian Creeds* p. 238.

Line 8. *God from God.* The use of the preposition "from" makes for a clearer as well as a more literal translation of the Greek *ek.* This whole phrase, repeated more fully in the next line, is retained to conform with the usual Latin and English versions. The fullness of expression also appears in the Greek text of the Creed of Nicaea, but "God from God" is absent in the Greek text of the so-called Creed of Nicaea-Constantinople, which is used in the liturgy. (Denzinger, *Enchiridion Symbolorum,* nos. 54, 86; also *Conciliorum Oecumenicorum Decreta,* Basle, 1962, p. 20.)

Line 10. The term *homoousios* is difficult to translate, but "Being" seems preferable to either "nature" or "essence" in a statement which tries to express the unity of the Godhead. Many consultants agreed that "Being" came nearest to the Greek philosophical term, even in its etymology. The argument of the sentence is that, because the Son is not made but begotten, he shares the same kind of being as the Father.

Line 11. This line makes it clear that the reference is still to the Son and not to the Father, and that he is the Father's agent in creation (cf. Hebrews 1:2).

Line 14. *by the power of the Holy Spirit.* The phrase safeguards the operation of the Holy Spirit in the incarnation, making it clear that no carnal activity is implied.

Line 17. *suffered, died.* The Greek *pathonta* is made to bear the notions of both suffering and death, cf. C. Mohrmann, *Etudes sur le latin des Chrétiens*, vol. 1, p. 210 on *passio.* Here it can also be reasonably argued that the inclusion of "died", as in the Apostles' Creed, provides a necessary and logical link between *passus* and *sepultus.*

Line 19. *in fulfilment of the Scriptures. Kata tas graphas* is again not an easy phrase to translate; but "in fulfilment of" was felt to be closer to the sense than "according to". The latter might suggest that Scripture says one thing, while other authorities say something different.

Line 20. *he ascended.* See the note on line 10 of the Apostles' Creed.

Line 21. *is seated.* This is preferred to "sits", to emphasize the permanence of Christ's position of honour.

Line 24. *the Lord, the giver of life.* These are two distinct phrases, both applying to the Holy Spirit. They avoid the possible misunderstanding of the older version "the Lord and giver", which might be taken to mean "the Lord of life" and "the giver of life".

Line 25. *and the Son.* This *Filioque* clause, which is a Western addition to the Creed, has been put in brackets as indicating that some Churches may include the words and other Churches may not. It was not considered to be within the province of this Committee to make recommendations as to its excision or retention.

Line 28. *We believe in one holy* . . . This phrase illustrates the need of reference to the Greek original, even for translation of the Latin. The latter here omits the preposition *in,* but *eis mian* in the Greek clearly requires "belief in" the Church, as well as "*in* God" and "*in* Christ". The word "holy" is also included in conformity with the Greek Text.

GLORIA IN EXCELSIS

1. Glory to God in the highest,
2.   and peace to his people on earth.

3. Lord God, heavenly King,
4. almighty God and Father,
5.   we worship you, we give you thanks,
6.   we praise you for your glory.

7. Lord Jesus Christ, only Son of the Father,
8. Lord God, Lamb of God,
9. you take away the sin of the world:
10.   have mercy on us;
11. you are seated at the right hand of the Father:
12.   receive our prayer.

13. For you alone are the Holy One,
14. you alone are the Lord,
15. you alone are the Most High,
16.   Jesus Christ,
17.   with the Holy Spirit,
18.   in the glory of God the Father. Amen.

The *Gloria in Excelsis* is a series of acclamations, a doxological and hymnodic form characteristic of the ancient Greek liturgies. Since it is not a dogmatic text, such as the creeds, a modern vernacular version may adapt its pattern to hymn structures that are more readily understood in English, without any basic modification of its substance and spirit. An analysis of the structure of the hymn shows that it consists of an opening antiphon based on St Luke 2:14, followed by three stanzas of acclamation, the first addressed to God the Father, the second and third to God the Son. The proposed translation of the text preserves this structure, but transposes certain lines and phrases for purposes of clarity and omits others to avoid unnecessary redundancy.

Lines 1–2. The text of this antiphon is uncertain in St Luke 2:14. The Eastern tradition refers the "favour" or "goodwill" to God, i.e. "God's peace and favour to men". But the Western tradition has generally read it otherwise—"God's peace among men of goodwill": or it may also be translated "God's peace among men of his favour". There is also the question as to whether "men" refers to mankind generally, or to the people of God who are the recipients of God's special favour. The proposed translation agrees with the consensus of New Testament scholars in the Revised Standard Version, the New English Bible and the Jerusalem Bible, that "favour" refers to God's favour; but it leaves open, in the phrase "to his people" whether "people" means all men or those who are specifically his people of faith and hope.

The translation of *in excelsis* is difficult. Literally, according to biblical imagery, it would mean "in the highest heavens". Today we do not have the mythological conception of a series of heavens, whether three or seven. It would be a simple solution to translate the phrase by "in heaven"; but this lacks the exultant feeling of the acclamation. The Revised Standard Version has therefore been adopted—"in the highest" —which agrees with older English Biblical versions and familiar liturgical and hymnodic usage.

Lines 3–6. This stanza is addressed to God the Father. The order of lines 3–4 and 5–6 in the original has been reversed, to make it clear at once to whom the acclamations refer. The Greek phrases "we bless you" and "we glorify you" have been omitted, since they are included in the words "worship", "thanks" and "praise". The stanza as now proposed consists of two pairs of parallel lines, coming to a climax in the word "glory".

Lines 7–12. This stanza is addressed to God the Son. The transposition of "only son of the Father" and "Lamb of God" in lines 7–8 gives to each of these lines an acclamation that praises Christ in both his divine and human natures; and it also places "Lamb of God" in immediate juxtaposition with what follows appropriately in lines 9–10. The common Greek version introduces "and Holy Spirit" after line 7, but this is a later displacement from line 17, as the Latin version makes clear. The double reference to Christ as "Son" in lines 7–8, which occurs in the Greek original, has been removed as redundant.

The declarative form has been preferred to the relative form in lines 9 and 11, as more suitable to acclamation. To avoid unnecessary repetition the three acclamations of lines 9–12 in the Greek text have been reduced to two. This is more logical: "have mercy on us" goes with line 9; and "receive our prayer" is related to Christ's session at God's right hand in line 11. The Greek manuscripts vary in the use of "sin" or "sins" in line 9. The singular has been adopted here, in accordance with the text of John 1:29.

Lines 13–18. The third stanza continues the acclamations to Christ. In order to effect the link the conjunction "for" is used. The repetition of "alone" is emphatic, to show that the titles here given to Christ are those which also belong to the Father– "Holy One, Lord, and Most High". Lines 16–18 are a concluding trinitarian doxology.

SANCTUS AND BENEDICTUS

1. Holy, holy, holy Lord, God of power and might,
2. heaven and earth are full of your glory.
3.   Hosanna in the highest.

4. Blessed is he who comes in the name of the Lord.
5.   Hosanna in the highest.

These texts are acclamations, based upon Scripture, but not exactly conforming to the texts of Isaiah 6:3 or St Mark 11:9–10 respectively. At an early stage in the Church's liturgical use the reference to "heaven" was added in line 2. The difficulty for the translator lies in the word *Sabaoth* of line 1, which literally means "heavenly hosts of angels", which Revelation 4:8 renders by *pantocrator*, "the Almighty". The common English translation of *Sabaoth* as "hosts" is open to misunderstanding, because of other associations of the word, while some people object to its military metaphor. The proposed translation, "God of power and might", seems to satisfy the meaning of the text in Isaiah and to avoid the misconceptions of popular Biblical and hymnodic versions.

As in the *Gloria in excelsis,* a further problem is a suitable translation of *in excelsis.* The Book of Common Prayer paraphrased line 3 by "Glory be to thee, O Lord most high". The version adopted here, "in the highest", conforms to that used in the *Gloria.* It has this advantage: the rhythm of the line in English is exactly the same as that of the Latin.

Because some liturgies do not use the *Benedictus* in immediate conjunction with the *Sanctus,* a space has been placed between the two texts.

GLORIA PATRI

1. Glory to the Father, and to the Son, and to the Holy Spirit:
2.   as in the beginning, so now, and for ever. Amen.

Line 1. The first part of the doxology is the more ancient and appears originally to have had the form *Gloria Patri per Filium in Spiritu Sancto.* In the fourth century, in opposition to those who claimed that this form expressed the Son's subordination to the Father, the form proposed in this line began to be used. The naming of the three Persons in parallel order agrees with the baptismal formula in St Matthew 28:19. This translation retains the first part in its traditional form since this was anciently regarded as setting forth doctrinal orthodoxy.

Line 2. The second part has developed from the simple response "for ever", first to include "now", and later — but only in the West—"as it was in the beginning". The Synod of Vaison in 529 considered the latter addition to be a protest against those who did not believe in the pre-existence of the Son. It has been pointed out that in this case the second half might apply not to "Glory" but to "the Son"; and that there is perhaps an intentional echo of John 1:1 in *sicut erat in principio.* It seems better to follow tradition, however, in taking "Glory" as the subject.

It is felt that the doxology's meaning is sufficiently clear without using the verbs commonly found in English versions. There are no verbs in the Greek form and only *erat* in the Latin.

SURSUM CORDA

1. The Lord be with you.
2. And also with you.

3. Lift up your hearts.
4. We lift them up to the Lord.

5. Let us give thanks to the Lord Our God.
6. It is right to give him thanks and praise.

Lines 1–2. The Committee is well aware of the problems which surround the translation of *Dominus vobiscum. Et cum spiritu tuo.* Some scholars, following van Unnik, would argue that "the Lord" refers to the Spirit; others, following Jungmann, believe that it refers to Christ. But after careful consideration of all the comments which have been received since the publication of the first edition of *Prayers we have in common,* the Committee has decided to retain the literal translation of *Dominus* - "the Lord", and to translate *cum spiritu tuo* simply as "and also with you".

Then there is the question of the verb. Should it be the indicative "is", or the subjunctive "be"? The versicle and response here are in the context of bidding and exhortation. Furthermore the subjunctive use in *Pax Domini sit semper vobiscum* would appear to indicate what the verb should be. There are also the greetings of St Paul in 1 Cor 16:23 and 2 Cor 13:13. Finally, the response of the people must be related to the greeting.

Lines 5–6. The Eucharistic Prayer is regarded as essentially an act of praise and thanksgiving to the Father. Following the basic Jewish prayer-form, the Christian liturgies blessed God by praising and thanking him for his works. *Gratias agamus* represents this underlying Hebrew concept and is therefore properly expressed, first by "Let us give thanks" and more fully by "it is right to give him thanks and praise". The use of "praise" at the end of the line gives the proper emphasis to the main thought.

AGNUS DEI

1. Jesus, Lamb of God:
2. have mercy on us.
3. Jesus, bearer of our sins:
4. have mercy on us.
5. Jesus, redeemer of the world:
6. give us your peace.

Since its introduction into the liturgy *Agnus Dei* has undergone a number of variations in Latin and vernacular forms. At first the one petition *miserere nobis* was unchanged at each repetition; but in the tenth and eleventh centuries it became common to substitute in the last line *dona nobis pacem.* It also became subject to variation in Requiems. The medieval period then gave rise to various Tropes on the anthem, which usually gave additional titles, but sometimes used phrases to bring out the meaning more clearly. In the Reformation liturgies of England and Germany *pacem* in line 6 was rendered "thy peace". The German form moreover prefixed the name "Christ" to each of lines 1, 3 and 5.

"Lamb of God", though full of meaning for those familiar with the biblical background in John 1:29, Isaiah 53:7, Revelation 5:6ff, etc, does not reveal this richness at first sight: but the Committee believes that the form now proposed does provide this more clearly and immediately. In the first place "Jesus" has been prefixed to "Lamb of God" at the beginning; and the name rather than the title is taken up again at the beginning of lines 3 and 5. Instead of the thrice-repeated relative clause *qui tollis peccata mundi,* a phrase is used in each of lines 3 and 5 to bring out the meaning of these words. The verb *tollis* can be interpreted "bear" or "take away"; and an attempt is made to render this dual meaning.

Line 6. *your peace.* This phrase not only gives a connection with John 14:27, but also with the *Pax Domini* in those rites, where *Agnus Dei* and *Pax Domini* are in juxtaposition.

The arrangement in six lines maintains the litanical structure.

TE DEUM

1. You are God: we praise you;
2. You are the Lord: we acclaim you;
3. You are the eternal Father:
4. All creation worships you.
5. To you all angels, all the powers of heaven,
6. Cherubim and Seraphim, sing in endless praise:
7.   Holy, holy, holy Lord, God of power and might.
8.   heaven and earth are full of your glory.
9. The glorious company of apostles praise you.
10. The noble fellowship of prophets praise you.
11. The white-robed army of martyrs praise you.
12. Throughout the world the holy Church acclaims you:
13.   Father, of majesty unbounded,
14.   your true and only Son, worthy of all worship,
15.   and the Holy Spirit, advocate and guide.
16. You, Christ, are the king of glory,
17. eternal Son of the Father.
18. When you became man to set us free
19. you did not shrink from the Virgin's womb.
20. You overcame the sting of death.
21. and opened the kingdom of heaven to all believers.
22. You are seated at God's right hand in glory.
23. We believe that you will come, and be our judge.
24.   Come then, Lord, to the help of your people,
25.   bought with the price of your own blood,
26.   and bring us with your saints
27.   to everlasting glory.

Versicle and Responses after the Te Deum

1. *V.*   Save your people, Lord, and bless your inheritance.
2. *R.*   Govern and uphold them now and always.
3. *V.*   Day by day we bless you.
4. *R.*   We praise your name for ever.
5. *V.*   Today, Lord, keep us from all sin.
6. *R.*   Have mercy on us, Lord, have mercy.
7. *V.*   Lord, show us your love and mercy;

8. *R.*   for we put our trust in you.
9. *V.*   In you, Lord, is our hope:
10. *R.*   May we never be confounded.

Like the *Gloria in Excelsis,* the *Te Deum* contains a series of acclamations which were highly stylised in their original Latin form. An attempt to produce a literal translation, maintaining the Latin word order, would result in something which would sound unidiomatic and odd: but where the Latin structure could be followed profitably, this has been attempted.

Lines 1–4 Here at the outset is the problem of translating the Latin triplets:

>   Te Deum laudamus:
>   te Dominum confitemur,
>   te aeternum Patrem: omnis terra veneratur.

The retention of these three acclamations in a parallel structure has much to commend it, not only from the point of clarity and incisiveness, but also as a poetic form. The vocative "O God" in the common English translation has no place in the Latin - which means literally "we praise you as God". *Terra* also means the whole cosmos and not just "earth".

Lines 7–8. See the notes on the Sanctus and Benedictus on Page 18.

Lines 13–15. A highly lyrical passage assisted in translation by inverting noun and adjective, "majesty unbounded", and the phrase "worthy of all worship" for the more prosaic "honourable".

The trinitarian ending of this section is clearly expressed. The Latin *paracletum* is not easy to translate: "comforter" has lost its original strong meaning; indeed no single English word was thought adequate, so "advocate and guide" have been used.

Line 16. This line begins the second section, which refers to the Son. Here there is a reminder of the question in Psalm 24, "Who is the King of Glory?" It is Christ.

Line 19. The Latin *horruisti* is not easy to translate in this context. Such words as "spurn, scorn and disdain" do not catch the idea of "dread" which must be conveyed. In spite of its other meanings, "shrink from" was generally thought to come close to the right meaning.

Line 20. *Devicto mortis aculeo.*   Some prefer to translate "draw the sting of death" rather than "neutralise the effects of the sting". The traditional word "overcome" covers both interpretations.

Line 24. The meaning of *subveni* is best expressed by a literal translation: "come to the help of".

Lines 26–27. "Bring us...glory" covers both the readings *munerari* (rewarded) and *numerari* (numbered).

Versicles and responses. The original text of the Te Deum ended at line 27; but traditionally it was followed by certain verses from the Psalms sung in the form of versicles and responses, which were known as *capitella.* The sources of these are as follows; **1–2** Psalm 28:10; **3–4** Psalm 142:2; **5–6** Psalm 123:3; **7–8** Psalm 57:1; **9–10** Psalm 71:1.

BENEDICTUS

1. Blessed be the Lord, the God of Israel;
2. he has come to his people and set them free.
3. He has raised up for us a mighty saviour,
4. born of the house of his servant David.
5. Through his holy prophets he promised of old
6.   that he would save us from our enemies,
7.   from the hands of all who hate us.
8. He promised to show mercy to our fathers
9. and to remember his holy covenant.
10. This was the oath he swore to our father Abraham:
11. to set us free from the hand of our enemies,
12. free to worship him without fear,
13. holy and righteous in his sight
14.   all the days of our life.

15. You, my child, shall be called the prophet of the Most High
16. for you will go before the Lord to prepare his way,
17. to give his people knowledge of salvation
18. by forgiving them their sins.
19. In the tender compassion of our God
20. the dawn from on high shall break upon us,
21. to shine on those who dwell in darkness and the shadow of
        death.
22. and to guide our feet on the road of peace.

Line 2. "Come to his people" more clearly renders *episkeptomai,* which is used for a coming which brings help, than does "visit" which suggests to modern ears something more casual. "Set them free" (echoed in line 11) with the N.E.B., is a more direct and modern phrase than a literal reproduction of *lutrosis,* such as "redemption".

Line 8. "He promised". The infinitive in Luke picks up the substance of the promise, and it is clearer if the "He promised" of line 5 is repeated.

Lines 10–14. In these lines Luke draws out the implications of the promise to Abraham, and a literal rendering would result in difficult English.

Line 11. Another word for deliverance is here also translated "to set free" for ease of rendering the lines which follow.

Line 12. The connection of the thought is made easier by repeating "free". "Worship" (with the N.E.B.) is, in this Lucan context, the proper translation of *latreuein*. Compare its use in Hebrews and Phil. 3:3.

Line 14. "All the days of our life" is intended by the text and gives a more complete and singable rhythm.

Line 15. "My child". The infant John Baptist is here addressed by his father.

Line 20. The better-attested reading—future tense instead of past— has been adopted. This is particularly suitable if the canticle is to precede the New Testament lesson instead of following it.

NUNC DIMITTIS

1. Now, Lord, you have kept your word:
2. let your servant go in peace.
3. With my own eyes I have seen the salvation
4. which you have prepared in the sight of every people:
5. a light to reveal you to the nations
6. and the glory of your people Israel.

This text from Luke presents few difficulties of interpretation.

Line 1. "Now" is emphatic and has therefore been placed at the beginning of the line. What is envisaged here and in line 2 is an owner/slave relationship. "Your word" refers back to the divine promise in Luke 2:26.

Line 2. "Let" contains the technical idea of manumission or discharge of a slave. In this case "death is the instrument of release" (Plummer). It is used in the Septuagint of the deaths of Abraham (Genesis 15:2), Aaron (Numbers 20:29), Tobit (Tobit 3:6) and others.
"In peace." This is also emphatic. The progression of major ideas in this couplet is maintained "Now...kept your word... let go...in peace".

Line 3. The introduction of a part of the body is typically Hebraic. The emphasis has been kept and Anglicised by the translation "with my own eyes".

Line 4. The emphasis of another Hebraism has been maintained by "in the sight of". The use of *laos* is difficult, particularly with the word *ethnōn* occurring in the next line. Even the plural of *laos* (cf. Acts 4:25-7) may mean Israel, but here it has been taken to mean the nations of the world. "Peoples" is no longer acceptable English, so the phrase "every people" is used.

Lines 5–6. "Light" and "glory" are taken to be in apposition to "salvation". The Messiah is the full shining of the shekinah or "glory" in the midst of his people Israel, and sheds universal light on the Gentiles.

27

The revelation which Christ brings needs more than a word like "lighten" or "illumine"; and, whilst avoiding the unsingable word "revelation", the idea has been retained in a verbal form.

"The nations"— an accurate translation of the word *ethnōn* would be "Gentiles" or "heathen" in apposition to Israel: but such words would be unacceptable in today's climate of thought—hence "nations".

MAGNIFICAT

1. My soul proclaims the greatness of the Lord,
2. my spirit rejoices in God my Saviour;
3. for he has looked with favour on his lowly servant,
4. and from this day all generations will call me blessed.
5. The Almighty has done great things for me:
6. holy is his Name.
7. He has mercy on those who fear him
8. in every generation.
9. He has shown the strength of his arm,
10. he has scattered the proud in their conceit.
11. He has cast down the mighty from their thrones,
12. and has lifted up the lowly.
13. He has filled the hungry with good things,
14. and has sent the rich away empty.
15. He has come to the help of his servant Israel
16. for he has remembered his promise of mercy,
17. the promise he made to our fathers,
18. to Abraham and his children for ever.

Line 1. The Greek has the idea of greatness in the verb, not in the object; and the familiar translation "magnify" expressed this: but it is archaic in this sense. The translation "proclaims the greatness" retains the idea of "greatness" though in a different place in the sentence.

Line 12. The word "lowly" comes from the same Greek root as "lowly" in line 3. It seems preferable to "humble and meek", both of which appear to have degenerated somewhat in popular usage.

Line 18. It is not entirely clear in the Greek whether the phrase "to Abraham and his children for ever" is in apposition to the phrase "to our fathers" in line 17; or whether it follows the phrase "remembered his promise of mercy" in line 16, with line 17 being parenthetical. Both alternatives remain open in this translation - the sense is the same in either case.